Rucksacks for the Leaf Cat

poems by

Dianna Henning

Finishing Line Press
Georgetown, Kentucky

Rucksacks for the Leaf Cat

Copyright © 2026 by Dianna Henning
ISBN 979-8-89990-330-4 First Edition
All rights reserved under International and Pan-American Copyright Conventions. No part of this book may be reproduced in any manner whatsoever without written permission from the publisher, except in the case of brief quotations embodied in critical articles and reviews.

Publisher: Leah Huete de Maines
Editor: Christen Kincaid
Cover Art: Manjula Leggett
Author Photo: Jody Wright
Cover Design: Elizabeth Maines McCleavy

Order online: www.finishinglinepress.com
also available on amazon.com

Author inquiries and mail orders:
Finishing Line Press
PO Box 1626
Georgetown, Kentucky 40324
USA

Contents

1. The Leaf Cat 1
The Star Drum 2
Scent of Solitude 3
Everything I hold dear was first made in the stars. 4
Angered by roadside carcasses, ... 5
Window Magic 6
All summer I've waited for 7
Half-Light of Twilight 8
The Day my Fallopian Tubes Asked Me to Play Hopscotch 9
In the Collage of My Mind I'm a Simple Design 10
My Face Washed Away in the Rain 11
On the Hood of the Tenuous 12
The Thick 13
Delivery 14
The Animals Will Indict Us 15
My knuckles are skulls. They make their beds under cold prayers. ... 16

2. Confession 17
The Christening Stone 18
Plate of Stone 19
Stirring up the Water 20
The Incandescence 21
Glass Garden Cloche 22
For the Love of Doorknobs 23
To Ask a Question Does Not Mean You Get an Answer 24
Trolling the Unknown 25
Already 26
When young, we stood naked in the rain. 27
The One with Violets in Her Lap 28
Sappho 1 29
Sappho 2 30
Magic Powder 31
Mitigation 32
I Once 33
What Remains 34
Missing You 35

3. Ultrasound 36
The Succulent 37
In the Aftermath of Afterwards 38
The Easel, the Leather Coat & the Blue Grass Perfume 39
The Sand Husband 40

Balancing the Books 41
At the Goodbye Door 42
Lovely that Black Crow Grandmother Brought into the Camp 43
Blood Relative 44
Ear Trouble 45
Fish Hatchery 46
Near the Now 47
From the Northeast Kingdom 48
Where Have All the Fishermen Gone? 49
Whiteout 50
New England Farmhouse 51

4. Search 52
How To Truth a Lie 53
My Heart's No Casual Affair, ... 54
Thieves, All of Them 55
To Nuance or Not to Nuance 56
Prison Portrait 58
Corralled in Queens 59
Fold your tears into peace signs. 60
Vice 61
The Whacking Stick 62
Summons 63
*The Trouble with Yesterday is That it's Not Today Even if it Plagiarizes
    Yesterday It Won't Be the Same.* 65

5. When the House Sleepwalks 66
Provisions 67
I Dare You 68
Birth Rights 69
Ever Since Her Cousin's Drowning 70
Sheep Dance 72
When a Day Trips You Up, Spits You Out 73
Anne Sexton as a Hologram 74
For the Dancing Birds 76
Tree Burial 77
When I am Dead and Shelved 78
What's dark remains dark 79
Can a Voice be Promiscuous? 80
To Measure Love with a Yardstick 81
The Opening World 82
At the Slightest 83

For those who believe in the magic of words

"What cannot be said will be wept."

—Sappho

"I, myself, from the very beginning,
Seemed to myself like someone's dream or delirium
Or a reflection in someone else's mirror,
Without flesh, without meaning, without a name."

—Anna Akhmatova

1. The Leaf Cat

If you stare at something long enough it assumes a life all its own.
Even the wind carries a child in a rucksack.
The child's name could be Leaf,
emblematic of green, its mixture of yellow and blue.
Our tortured world loves green,
its promise of better times.
Oh, to be green in the long night of terror.
Meanwhile, the leaf-cat reclines on a padded porch chair.
The cry in its throat is red.

The Star Drum

Who's astonished by the way
stars smell like communion wafers?

Already the galaxy's priests
have rounded up the runaways.

Whoever has ash on their tongue
is doubly blessed. There once

was a drummer boy
whose drumstick had eyes.

Every star he ever paddled
carried a scent of water.

Whoever speaks in stars
has a steel drum for a heart.

Percussion is a matter of attunement.

Scent of Solitude

There was a doe that hobbled onto the front porch, her hoof mangled.
There was her fawn that followed.

Both ate from the cat's bowl.

I was alone watching this,
sipping coffee by the window. Hunger followed both animals.

Their hunger howled like coyotes in moonlight.

The world stopped as they ate.
A scent of quiet just before things bloom.

The doe stepped back to let her fawn have his fill.
She was dying inside herself.

There was a prayer she uttered as she watched her offspring.
A cadence that made the house bend towards her.

She was more than her body returning to the woods.
She burst into radiant being.

You could hear the gods beating their drums.
You could smell the scent of their solitude.

Everything I hold dear
was first made in the stars.

I wonder where you are
in the Vast that refuses my entry. I would

reach out, touch you, but death's finality
is a bitch. When my dog chases

cows, she turns, smiles as I yell Come.

I like to think of you smiling
as you speed through infinity. Please hold me

again, so I'll forget which side of me you left. I want
to feel your embrace, your breath on my temple.

Angered by roadside carcasses,

how their bellies swell in heat,
heads tilted back

as though in wonder
over the marvel of death,

or their view of the eternal,
how it splashes onto the living,

and I shiver into the steering wheel,
grip it tighter as though life

could be held onto forever.

*

Not until one's grasp
relaxes does the blurring begin—

the insignificant self
plotting against time,

her recklessness at being alive.

Window Magic

A doe stretches
to reach the topmost
leaves as she strips
our Mock Orange bush,
nose wet as a dew-
dipped blackberry.

She doesn't know
I lean into the kitchen sink,
crane to catch
her every movement.

I won't knock
on the window,
even though
this fragrant shrub
she grazes on is my favorite.

Tonight,
I'll let stars wash me clean,
dream of deer,
how such gazing
blossoms into happiness.

All summer I've waited for

things to go up in fiery plumes,
the errant brightness of burn piles—
lick and talk of things grown hot.

~~~

Trace me back to the look on your face
when you heard me read
Heat in the Noonday Shade.

In the foreskin of desire,
a new grief flowers:
we were perfect for each other,
your eyes caught fire.

We cleared our land to find each other.
We built our burn piles higher.

Half-Light of Twilight

The mountain presses itself into the sky.
They are lovers,
the mountain more aggressive.

There's always one to lead,
that first flowering of passion at top speed.

Like how we curled up by the Yuba River,
both of us entwined on our blanket.

>	O, the season of it
>	O, the heights

The years crack open their nutshells.
Now for our meaty savoring.

The Day my Fallopian Tubes Asked
Me to Play Hopscotch

The fire carries on with the logs.
Clearly there's something going on between them.

Like when we first met and harvested each other,
not with fire rather with flesh.

If our lives are stanza breaks,
little rooms inside a house,

can we really discern
which room we'll next enter?

—Go ahead. Pin a dance on me.
I'm turning into an Autumn leaf—

The day my fallopian tubes asked
me to play hopscotch is

the day my rambunctious expletives
burst into lava flows.

In the Collage of My Mind
I'm a Simple Design

The years are rapt birds,
trilling their delight,

no salt on their tongues
no weights on their wings,

no rambunctious expletives
in their voices,

not a single lofty sermon, only
the width of stars in their throats.

My throat is a winding river,
where words carry me

into the sanctity of all that flows
no matter flood or drought.

I've learned to listen with my mouth.
To make words with wings.

To carry myself without fear of what's ahead.

My Face Washed Away in the Rain

Caught in the streetcorner's drain,
crumpled papier-mâché.

A mask perhaps.

I was always a mask,
seeking refuge behind hills,
trees, a glass of wine.

When the gutter's
herringbone of Pennzoil
slicks my mask
with rainbow streaks,
I scrub it clean.

      The asphyxiation of perfection,
its fetid stench, how it grooms the future.

On the Hood of the Tenuous

Nights grow dangerous with owls.

A thump against the windshield,
a flurry of feathers
that become blood glued
to the windshield,

then this realization:

*it could have been me
blinded by headlights.*

Between one door and the next
there's a lucid opening:

the bird's or my borrowed body
staked in the tenuous.

The Thick

Birds peck sod from your head.

You tell them that the worm
of thought is buried deep,
that the infinite is beside the point.

(It's not true that any nest will do.
Some fare better than others.)

When a rainstorm presses in,
the crow grows raucous,
wakes the neighborhood,
each house a night-lantern.

Pecking through sod is not like
standing on the rim of the infinite.

Crows wear night to become invisible.
Daybreak, one struts, preens his feathers.

Dark's no trouble, except when
you're in the thick of it.

Delivery
  (Hemiceratoides hieroglyphica)

Moths from Madagascar
drink tears from the eyes
of sleeping birds,
a small saucepan of socket
acting as well,

the moths' proboscis
dipping in to sip
from the slumbering. Nightly,
I close my eyes
hoping no moth flutters down
to quench its thirst. What's

feared is the unknown,
the way death of anything
becomes a hoodlum stalker
dishing up surprise.

The Animals Will Indict Us

With burnt paws, flames riding bareback,
bears raced down mountainsides,
pines crackling, trunks snapping,

the unholy terror of destruction, infernos
engulfing trees, vegetation, animals,
ground and rocks blackened
into vestments priest's wear—

the stench of ash as though all of earth
was burial ground   and perhaps so,
death upon the dead, mounds of them,
the aching back of earth weighted with so many bones,
what to do with so many,

and who'll cry for the land, the animals, the people,
who'll extinguish the harm wrought,
or right balance with a good shepherd's eye?

My knuckles are skulls.
They make their beds under cold prayers.

The spend-thrift heart
won't budge an iota,
and that wrap of nosegays

you left for me between
the screen and front door
is squandered in winter.

Already, sleep's a bear,
its bleak and heavy slippage
into nowhere important.

Really, no one steadies
the wind's machinations,
and there's no accounting
for frozen flowers.

2. Confession

The lilies of my life have always been ghosts
waiting in the Netherworld
with fingers beckoning:

"Strumpet, we tempt you,"
their tongues slavered with hope.

*

Who recalls the pond at Giverny,
how the lovely bridge
arched like a stroked cat?

Monet found
pleasure of the eye…
motifs to paint,
while I saw water as hypnotic.

*

Not even a lunge,
no matter how well-conceived,
could permanently dunk me.

*

This is not rubbish.

This is confession:

I so loved the water that so loved me,
and I took from the lilies my life—my new life.

The Christening Stone

There's only one stone
that matters. Cushioned in mud
and clay and seaweed,
it feeds on dreams.

In the sludge
of spring's first run-off,
a hand might reach down,
lift the nearby weight of one,
skip it across water's
irrepressible bone. Who
has picked such a stone
from amongst the many?

And why that one?

I was once touched
by such a stone and because
of that I turned human.

But first, I was stone.

Plate of Stone

On grass
I placed a plate of stone.
No birds drank from it,

nor errant cats
on sly intent,
nor did deer,

often evident
this time of year,
lap their reflected edge.

So cool was this
plate of stone,
its scant profile

on the lawn,
that it might have been
a blackbird

basking in the sun,
were it not
for the fact stone

was all I heaped
upon my plate.

Stirring up the Water

A woman stacks her clothes
in a large willow basket after washing

them in the nearby brook,
her husband's shirt neatly folded

on top of the laundry.

When a residue of soap slips off
her wedding band,

she drops to her belly on the bridge,
her hands churning up mud,

waves rocking the brookweed.
Above her, a handful of airy birds,

steady on their kites of wind,
circle to watch as she stirs

the water, fingers probing stones,
alongside velveteen contours.

She could be a courtesan,
prostrate before her master,

who asks, as did Lady Murasaki,
"What has the future in store for me?"

The grief of loss is the grief of centuries—
a wedding band slipped off,

a stone chipped from rock.

The Incandescence

From my bath
I step into the chilly air.
Droplets cascade
down my legs,
my towel absorbing them.

I think of May,
how everything
greens to blossom,
then burnishes

by mid-October
to papery lanterns,
husks of flowers,

everything becoming
memory's incandescence.

*

Who leans against the window
as if to recline
against the moon,

breathing embers
into flame as she dries?

Here in the dark,
where all things gravitate
towards silence,

shines a spotlight, its arch
mooring in the sky.

Glass Garden Cloche

My neighbor takes a knee
as though to pray
while fitting glass bells
over leafy sprigs
fresh as a baby's skin.

Each morning
he cuts across our yard to work
where seeds fasten
in their rows.

I walk over, stand
by him, watch
as he carefully lifts
each portable greenhouse.

Struck by what comes up
he leans to cup
each tomato sprig as he might
a woman's breast.

The world could tremble for this.

The soil could translate our lives
by how we bend,
fasten things to earth.

For the Love of Doorknobs

There's the beveled glass kind with rosettes or sunbursts
that massage your hand
as you saunter into another room,

white porcelain ones that remind you of bathrooms,
their spotless marble,
lavatories that belie bodily functions,

as well as antique brass openers
that slip like wet lollipops
from your hand,

or the fancy Brittany or Flanders kind—more ostentatious
than usual,
black Georgian knob sets

sedate as nuns in their veils,
and you marvel that your hand holds
all the other hands that have opened doors,

but the very best handles are wooden knobs
that tell stories of the wind
caressing trees before they were chopped

and how each bent as to bow
to this earth they loved.

To Ask a Question Does Not Mean You Get an Answer

All winter I remained with the dead, a white haired
old woman, knuckles big
as dollops of honey. Asked

my name by a nurse's aide, I couldn't
remember, instead I recalled a river
where my lover and I once swam. *The Winooski,*

I answered causing the aide
to wrinkle his nose. I fished
for a rose from my nightgown. *The dead*

are in rehearsal, I told his half
shut eye. That's when he hustled
down the hall to fetch a doctor.

Floodgates opened. The observation room
swayed with seaweed. If anyone
asks, I'm swimming across the ocean

to Bethlehem. I want to hear
the sermon on the Mount, or at the very least
touch Mary Magdalene's hem.

Trolling the Unknown

A handsome God trolling the universe drops by,
sits beside you at the dinner table. He's not
well versed in poetry but knows tons about myth.

Pieces of your spaghetti ship off for Alaska,
and the puzzled God asks, *Where the hell's Alaska?*
With little hope of illuminating him on earth's geography,

you stick to your solar system and reply, *Far off as Neptune.*
He fondly speaks of Neptune's rapturous winds
and inquires, *Do you want to troll the unknown with me?*

Your response, perhaps curt, implies you
already troll the unknown using nymphs as bait,
your spaghetti reminding you it's no worm.

Such a wise guy this God who lectures, *Line control*
is a problem with nymphs. Fed up, and somewhat well fed,
escape is your only option. You've been outwitted,

and you determine that the next time you dine
with a God you'd best brush up on your angler techniques.

Already

Touch me in the night of my body.
Where the wind can't get in.
Where rose petals turn magenta.

Already I have loved you, have left you.
What remains is that which cannot be spoken.
The other day I heard a wind speak your name.

The willow branches seared my arm
as I walked where we'd once walked.
I remember you because I cannot forget.

Already my loneliness is dark with grief.
Nothing remembered that can't be retrieved.
Your hand rested in mine in my sleep.

Already my body is a homecoming.
I'll wait for you on the front stoop near the lilacs.
In the distance your footsteps grow louder.

When young, we stood naked in the rain.

Inside our VT cabin we towel dried each other,
scent of the earth in our hair.

How many millennia does it take to get back
to a second chance, another go at it?

You made oatmeal porridge for breakfast
while I picked blackberries from the nearby field.

Each berry you popped in my mouth
tasted sweet as our first kiss.

If I hadn't left you forty years ago
would we still be standing in the rain?

Such discovery one makes in the other.
You were my lover, and I loved you.

The One with Violets in Her Lap

If she were someone else's sister
I'd again make her mine,
twist her bones
into recognition—
the catacombs of her eyes,
deep and memorable.

If she were lost
I'd surely find her,
coax her back,
the same way she returned
with each push
on the playground swing.

My studio clock,
a mercenary,
intones its message.

She won't return.

The one who survives
is the one left behind.

                    (Title from Sappho)

Sappho 1

    You tasted moon flesh,

swallowed its sweetness,
settled back on feathered pillows

    to watch stars float
across night's benevolence

Cleis, why leave me with such sorrow?

    *

    Now even candlelight sucks
as it gloms onto the wick

    *

Since you left, I've learned
to enter rock with my breath, to bury
    that old bone grief

Sappho 2

Fetch me my papyrus scroll
        I must write of her lithe body,
                breasts golden as honey,
                        garlands in her hair

———

Blessed Goddess,
    let her stay longer,
do not rip her from my arms

———

        I ache for her again and again

———

Adonis, hear this!

I've joined the covenant of women
        in whom no man sleeps,
                nor rakes aside

Magic Powder

Kingfisher, fetch me my voice.
I swallowed it with tears
and ginseng tea.

My work has become wooden
and there's heartworm
on its dark veneer.

"Look for magic powder
underneath a bird's wing,"
grandmother said.

I'd watch, hours at a time,
Kingfishers scout for minnows,
and wonder why brook-water
didn't wash powder off the birds.

Whenever I took a bird bath
at her house,
I'd scrub underneath my gooseflesh arms,
quickly towel dry.

Afterwards, I'd open the round container
of her rose scented powder,
pat it underneath my arms,
clouds of talc falling to my feet.

Then I was both bird and human
made from my own magic,
and I could sometimes speak
in the manner of angels.

Mitigation

When the Spanish Maja Dusting powder
box slipped from her fingers,
spilling onto the floor,

she quickly got on her knees,
a washcloth in hand,
but no matter how hard

she scrubbed to lift powder
off the floor, it spread
like a contagion, the sweet scent

of geranium, carnation, and patchouli
escaping underneath the bathroom door.
Her hands, fraught with worry

Grandmother might scold her.
How could she have known
that her grandmother would rejoice

over such curiosity, that she, too, once
spilled her grandmother's Yardley
English Lavender powder and found

in the floor's miniature swirls
such magic as befits extraordinary dreams:
fairy dust mitigating curiosity.

I Once

had a sister close as my breath.
She fell asleep on the beach and the ocean took her.

What mythic Selkie sprang from that water,
to capture what I'd loved, cherished? Already

my arms are longing filled with seizures,
sand-dunes warm where she'd slumbered.

The water's edge surrounds my toes, as I belt out
her name. But nothing rises from the sea.

In the watery depths her hair splays in the current.
I imagine the late-night moon as her dance partner.

Dawn gouges me. *I should have said, I should have done.*
Nowhere in my life have I burned more thoroughly than in hindsight.

What Remains

My sister's hand splits from mine.
Breathless, I cannot catch up to her.

Only a tattered scarf
from her insistent flight,

its torn fringes remain
threaded between my fingers.

At night, I call out her name
and search the darkened

corridors of grief. If you
should happen to see her,

please, I insist, tell her
someone's looking for her.

If she no longer wants to see me, tell me nothing.

Missing You

I sometimes
press my hand
to my heart
as though
it was your heart.

Such is the way
I continue to live
without you. Who

makes her body
ready for grief
by keeping frayed

letters, their scent
carefully tucked
in an embossed
stationary box?

They're soft as flannel
and smell of wind.

Their sleeves,
an open kimono.

3. Ultrasound

My husband lies on an elevated bed
while a technician dips her wand
into slippery gel to glide across
his chest. The room is dark. Only

a monitor registers streams of light
that glow red, blue, and yellow. Inside
my husband's heart there's a temple.
He grows silent at its opened door.

The stillness around us sails
rough waters, interrupted only
by the monitor's whoosh and burp.
We say nothing in the examining room.

Instead, we look at what's to come,
one leaving, the other leaving later
and the stillness that speaks
of loss and more loss.

The Succulent

Was it was the slope of his shoulder
as he slept, how the vulnerable spine

becomes stem to some exotic fruit
that enticed me to burrow into him,

or the way the pupil floats underneath
the eye's foreskin, one thing

resembling something else? We spat,
and I'd shouted the irreverent,

I want to split. Running away
had been my fait accompli,

but recently its appeal lessened,
realizing I tussle mostly with myself.

Instead of running off, I closed
the space between us, my breath,

soughing down his back. "You're
perfectly imperfect," I remind myself.

In the Aftermath of Afterwards

The leash snaked home behind the dog. But
my husband out walking our Samoyed was missing.
(Who wonders if darkness is evaporation?)

Lily, spooked, sped inside, shook off snow,
her tongue long as a man's necktie,
our *Trailblazer* flashlight, nowhere in sight.

Where was the man who'd walked her?
Sammy's tail fanned the room. She barked.
I said *Quiet, where is he?* Fear,

a prelude to the unimaginable. Perhaps
his heart burst and he's a heap in a snowbank.
Nighttime drivers can't easily discern

one shadow from the next. He might
have looked like rabbit brush or perhaps
a friend picked him up, took him for a beer.

I lock Lily in her metal crate,
slip on my jacket, walk out his route.
The wind slaps my back, I punch it back.

My screaming out his name
renders zilch—blizzardly snow of dancing
dervishes. I hightail it home. The man

I'd frantically looked for opens the door.
Where the hell have you been, he asks. Adding,

*"I know you like to make snow men,
but really, darling, in this weather?"*

The Easel, the Leather Coat & the Blue Grass Perfume

Which was given first, who remembers?
It was Christmas and the house demurred.

You, my Then Husband, pinched open a window,
said, *Let's cut us a tree*. We drove to the woods

near Huntington, Vermont and parked our Renault,
boots filling with clunky snow.

I followed you, or was it the ax I followed?
Its blade shadowed against snowdrifts,

a sinister smile alongside its edge. Ahead,
rows of balsam firs, snow flecked.

You ungloved your hand, leaned into the ax.
"How about this one?" I nodded yes.

It didn't take long to fell the tree, so we slogged
back to our car with a roped fir secured to our sled.

Back home you sawed boards, nailed them to the balsam's
base, stood the tree upright in our college apartment.

We cut out decorations from construction paper,
made an angel from cotton balls. All the while I mourned

our young age, a child on the way; it seemed I'd come
to a brick wall. You stood on a stepstool, latched

our angel to the top plume. So much regret, but
when I left you years later, I didn't leave anything behind.

Who opened first? I no longer recall my gifts to you.
At a friend's, you'd made me a pine easel.

So often, I've tried to paint you, fix you better in mind.
The leather coat went to the thrift. I no longer wear perfume.

The Sand Husband

"Dare you to follow," I taunted,
tossing my towel onto the back of the chaise,

my toes dipping into the sea,
"I'm in before you."

This was and wasn't the case.

Because he was the Sand Husband,
I didn't associate him with time.

But I am neither swimmer
nor dreamer. I wade out only so far

and return to bury my head in the sand,
regretting his loss, how casually I let him go.

Balancing the Books

Sound is a star I hang onto
when night balances its books.

In dreams, I polish the stone of myself
in the clear water of memory.

You once spoke of loss,
how it subtracts.

Didn't we believe our marriage
was more than a tithe,
that we'd always be together?

The salve of my heart is bonemeal.
This tightrope keeps me steady.

At the Goodbye Door

Wind knocks on your door; a mackintosh
slung over its arm, a sigh like coyotes

as they grate their teeth, their rheumy eyes contagious
with stars, tongues slavered with hope—

their coats reminiscent of ones you donated to the thrift,
collars roughed up, delicate threads a reminder of what binds—

how we were together long enough to retrieve the inexplicable.
Satiated, we purged ourselves: You at the goodbye door,

me sweeping the floor where you stood and always a crooner
in the background singing, *Love's a Difficult Wing.*

Lovely that Black Crow
Grandmother Brought into the Camp

Years later, my grandfather
reached into his pocket for a handkerchief
and extracted my grandmother like a molar from the grave

There's no exception to the strangeness
in some families, mine no exception

Now my grandfather's bed is a barge
that floats from dream to dream

He's unlikely to rise for prayers
His oldest daughter continues to carry him a milk jar
filled with sipping cream

and the crow that was a harbinger
lies buried in a shoe grandfather
will never again wear

Blood Relative

I never knew my tall, winsome Aunt Winona, her
arms a fine bone China, face
a Modigliani; someone who might
have recited Keats or Robert Burns, perhaps pressed
roses in a family Bible along with divorce filings. What

she smelled of, not a hint, her voice, no trace. In the only
photo, her holding me in infancy, there's
a clue: her gaze stuck
between ahead and behind—pretty
woman with a bobbed cut. Her satin, A-line dress

slack over the cliff of her hips; her wedge shoes, Suiter
Hat with black veil, all speaking a certain
respectability—small ruby necklace, a blood stain,
resting in the hollow of her throat; a premonition
to blood clots she'd later die from. Given Winona's

necklace years after she passed, I often wore it, until
one day, taking an outdoor shower, I soaped
the spot it rested in, groped for the familiar chain, searched
drain-rocks, and understood that I held loss as though
it was the only stable thing to hold when a woman decides enough.

Ear Trouble

When a child misbehaved,
it was always the ear
she first grabbed.

At the time
I wondered if their ears
would grow into misshapen flowers,
if an ear could seek refuge
in a secret hideout.

Whenever she approached me,
I'd duck,
run the opposite way.
It wasn't easy to read her intention.

I wondered how the ears slept at night,
what comfort they took from darkness—
or if by morning they'd look like
crushed Dahlia piñatas.

Fish Hatchery

My but we were lovely, captives
and all. Each day mother

dressed us up. She was keeping us
for herself. And we kept to the fish-

hatchery, where shadows stacked
their hieroglyphs. Cautiously, we

eyed ripples in the murky tanks
where fingerlings thinned

into nearly nothing. Each day
she would dress us up, twist

our hair into ringlets, bangs pinched back
with plastic barrettes. Oh, we were lovely

until we held our own, asserting no more
taffeta dresses, no more ringlets,

our arms defiantly across our chests,
my foot booting the cat.

Near the Now

The orchard owner instructed apples were best kept
individually wrapped in newspaper,
stored in a cool place. Tenderly wrapping them,

we sat across from each other, husband, and wife,
cautious lest we bruise one. Content, we remained silent,
as though we could read not the newsprint,

rather each other. After twenty years together,
words become a sideshow, and didn't we delight we'd secured
fruit for winter—for ourselves and for our children?

How long ago we stored for winter no longer matters.
Frostbite killed the following year's yield,
so, we didn't go apple picking. But perhaps we're still

in the orchard and you're holding firm the ladder
while I navigate branches. We might be thinking of apple pie,
or mason jars filled with apple butter.

But we'd called it quits. You went your way,
I mine, so there was no preserving that year,
yet, still, you steady the ladder.

From the Northeast Kingdom

1

When the black bearskin hung from the tree
like a rug drying on the clothesline,

the hunter recounted how he started an incision
below the anus, cut upward to the head,

stopped at the mouth's corners. *From the rear paws
I cut to the elbow, crossed to the chest incision,*

his voice razzed the youngster who watched,
Are you sickward, Child? It wasn't until he

got to the head that fuzziness rocked her.
Between kerosene kerplunking into the cook-

stove, and her grandfather's graveled voice,
she silently wept for the ears turned

inside out, pressed back. The bear's

2

life spoke to her of fresh droplets
coating his fur tips, and the scent of blackberries rose.

Inside his choice thicket, he reaches for vines,
and pulls leaves, thorns, berries towards him,

meshing them into his mouth—such sweetness.
Only when he satiates himself,

turning in his dark poetic cape does the hunter
bring him down—a moment of beauty and satisfaction

supremely merged, and he falls,
as only a black bear falls, king

of his forest, crowned by rainfall.

Where Have All the Fishermen Gone?

The camp door slammed, the men's fishing gear
in hand as they raced for their rowboats, shoved off

the lake's shore, Kentucky tobacco pouches
bulging pockets, home brew tucked in gray coveralls.

They fish 'til nightfall, heft their pails back onto
shore, tell the women folk; *We wrestled the orneriest*

fish and by Jove, wouldn't you know, it slipped
the hook. Biggest Largemouth Bass this side of Morgan.

What patience did I have, while they fished, at my easel
eking visions, I had no training for; the wormy paint

squeezed from derelict tubes so silver they'd slip my fingers—
dried paint mucking my palate knife? Sometimes

a vision evaporates, too large to execute:
Stubborn, I piled layers of paint

over mistakes until the canvas's weight
toppled the easel. How like fishing is art. You wade

through treacherous streams struck by something,
the water deep, murky, sometimes roiling.

Whiteout

A dozen gutted rainbows in the Ziploc
sleepily curve into each other.
They're no longer privy to secrets
of a pebble-lined riverbed
nor can they watch rain cast its line.

Years back I'd press my forehead
against the boat's empty seat,
watch the struggling pink gills
fan open and shut, my Vermont
grandfather's blows on their steely heads

hardly enough to keep them
from believing air might somehow
replenish them as they sucked
deeper into the whiteout of death.

Such heady curiosity, my two poking fingers
hooking into their contracting gills
as though I were entering the woman of myself.

New England Farmhouse

Down from Bob Ovitt's place, two sisters linger
at their clothesline to watch as the farmer's two hundred
eighty-pound body is hoisted into a flatbed and then
driven in a scrawl of dust around the bend. These
sisters, legendary for their efficiency, are later asked
by the town-clerk to sort through their neighbor's papers,
a task each accomplished after their husbands died—one
from a tractor spill, the other from a virus. For years
they've lived together in a harmony of thought. October

both amble up to Ovitt's farmhouse to sort
his papers. Etta, the eldest, shoulders open
the door. They look around before attacking mounds
of mail on the cider-ringed table. Outside,
winds churn poplar leaves, causing Etta
to ponder their sixty-two-year-old neighbor, who lay
dead days before anyone suspected. She's more
attuned to the quirks of fate and visualizes Bob gagging
on a chicken bone, his ruddy hands hacking at his throat

to dislodge the shard. She wonders if the draft
around her shoulders is his rank
breath: if the dead, out of longing, draw close, waiting
for someone to tug them back. Her sister extracts
from an envelope, a letter Bob wrote but didn't mail, and reads it
aloud: *Chopped down trees in the north pasture to increase
my view of your place. Still, no word from you.* Etta covers
her mouth and indicates *No More*. She's not
mentioned Bob's indiscretion, how
he cupped her buttocks when she carried up his supper.

4. Search

Mother once told me my wakefulness took
up an entire floor—that's

why I house myself in the woods. All
the tree knows of cover is moss. All

the child in Ukraine knows of cover is run. I can't
reconcile what's happening in the world. Night

leavens its darkness, buried
in hypocrisy and vile

politicians. There's a fog
catcher in Lima who brings water

to the poor. I've asked him
to speak to us.

How To Truth a Lie

Because a newborn fawn settles on his knees in a bed of pine needles
        to nurse under the roof of his mother

Because the war-torn world is in shambles,
        yet, still, I believe small miracles will appease the demonic

Because sunshine pours through the ponderosa's needles
        threading sunlight across our mountainous terrain

Because my pulse tells me *You're alive, and you breathe in the lives of others*
        & they matter: a mother in Gaza, her child, the toddler blasted in Kiev

Because to obliterate a lie truth must be told time and again,
        until the lie is a shrunken corpse decomposing under its own weight

Because I must believe that the world begs we see it in the light of love,
        that we, finally, rest our heads on the pillows of peace

My Heart's No Casual Affair,

never a skip roping freak,
nor does it invite curious spectators

to chant those jumping songs
we memorized as children. No,

my heart seeks peace in a world gone
awry; nineteen school children

and two teachers killed in Texas,
war in Ukraine, a madman's dream.

There once were lilacs growing
outside my window. This year they've become
rusted tea bags, little starvelings.

Thieves, All of Them
              (Because of the Pandemic)

The bandits barged into homes while the people were sick,
heedless of posted *Stay Away* signs.
Their hands were razor sharp.

They wore socks over their shoes.
No sound emanated from their footsteps.

Thousands died from a mysterious illness,
their bodies hauled away.
No one kept ledgers of the diseased.

It was as though they'd never lived.
Only the robbers thrived,
building up their bank accounts.

Tell the people that locking their doors does no good.
That the earth continues to get about on a prosthetic.

Tears are dung. Stinking dung.

To Nuance or Not to Nuance

*

The men I worked with at Folsom Prison,
walk single line
down the knife of night,
their eyes averted,
their blue jeans baggy

They could be on their way
to chapel,
Bibles in their hands,
and who knows what
in their back pockets

*

My drama instructor knows the poetry
of the body, each nuance a shift;
he lifts the sloping shoulders of one prisoner,
teases his mouth into a smile

"….I could be bounded in a nut-shell and count
myself a king of infinite space, were it not
that I have bad dreams."

*

In my dream, I am a frog leaping into heaven,
a moth perched on my tongue—
cool lake water glistening
off the green which is my frogness

Oh, Holy Father of leaping things
give me dominion over myself,
as well as those that wrestle
with hope's illusive pond

Please bless these men who remain
chastised by public curse, by accusations,
some of which are legally true

*

I once thought trouble
a blight on the spirit,
but trouble is a shapeshifter
it smiles like an angel,
dresses in shadowy garb

*

"Hamlet is like ballet,"
said the inmate in Arts in Corrections.
"How so?" I asked.

"It's all such delicate stuff."

Prison Portrait

Housed in a cell, the soul
squats in a cement corner.

It hums like the defunct hanging
alcoves of Old Folsom.

Some men break down,
while a few, mostly the young
make do with the salt
and bread of labor.

Each day a gray wipe-out
in the State's fortress.

Concertina wire twangs.
It's no dance tune. Prisoners know

work boots aren't made for dancing,
nor do shackled feet shuffle

to any old razzamatazz.

Corralled in Queens

Someone must have phoned the cow,
informed her the slaughterhouse
was around the corner,

so, she bolted
through the stockyard
into the world of humans,
her trotters clicking,
eyes scouring for hideouts,

and soon a scream of sirens
assaulted her,
streets jammed with cop cars,
and she couldn't second guess
patrol officers,

their unusual interest
in her. Were they baffled
by her girth,
her beauty, beauty being
a tinker's toy?

So, she fled down Elm.

**

When this was reported
by the media
people wanted to know if
she was awarded a reprieve—

after all, so much muscular effort
should reap reward,
stall death rather than be stalled.

Fold your tears into peace signs.

When your neighbor is the enemy
and night pulls its sharpened knife,

a word does what a word must.
It summons its bloodhounds.

Wheat fields turn barren.
An old woman pours seeds

into a soldier's jacket pocket.
When he's later shot down

sunflowers will blossom his gravesite.
(Beauty's reprieve in mayhem.)

Sooty debris smudges streets.
Neither the notations of loss, nor

the uncompromising hand of indifference
assuages the survivors. War's a thug who sucks

his thumb in a limousine's backseat
and gorges on caviar.

Vice

> *"My home is burning, my homeland*
> *Is bleeding, and therefore I am."* -Bohdan Andrukh

It happened one night, perhaps more often,
that a sleeping Canadian Goose
at the *Honey Lake Wildlife Refuge*
hadn't felt the trap-ice
creep in around her body
holding her prisoner, unable
to flap free. So, when the coyote,

tongue hanging like a torn rag,
gingerly crept up, circled around
the bird, the goose awakened,
frantically powered up to free herself,
ice becoming blood's crazed map.

So it is that Putin entraps
thousands, borders sealed.
Citizens hiding in subway tunnels
the fortunate unharmed.

A double-headed eagle
depicts empire, while Ukraine's
national bird, the nightingale
sings. We, in other countries,
are left with a sorrow so large it avoids
the geography of comprehension.

Listen, listen, the nightingale sings,
my fatherland is burning, my heart scorched.

The Whacking Stick

A boy with a long stick whacks the air.
What demon does he strike?

How little it takes to make a child,
set him loose upon the world.

The bruised air makes no reply.
Docile and submissive it stands abuse.

The nine-year-old goes on striking what he can't have,
what he doesn't miss since never having.

He'll grow up, take revenge on someone,
perhaps his own child.

No one can tell him to stop whacking.
The uncompromising hand of his father stained to his cheek.

Summons

1

This is my cutting board. These
are my hands adept at cutting. This
is my chicken whose neck I'll sever.

My cutting board floods with new
geographies. I pluck my fingers of blood. Who

knows a woman's aim when she swings?
The word-hands of the world lay wreaths

at the serifs of despair. Who says
it can't be done? The potted
chicken boils and bubbles,
my poem, with time, rights itself.

This is my cutting board.
These are my hands. What happens

2

when it's over remains,

this indenture to memory. Today, taste of your skin
suffices. Salt enters the bloodstream.

Don't take me for a mad woman or shrew.
All day I've stirred. Yesterday, the river over-flowed

as we reclined on groundcover.
May I? May I, you'd asked. The river answered.

Already, I swoon in recall
of the Yuba, its fluctuance, its greed. He almost

(cont.)

3

swallowed me with his fame,
but I'm a sound woman and kept in mind:
I will, by sheer will, one day equal or surpass you.

Such belief is how a woman survives the Dominate.

That's why my rock finally threw its punch.
You only lack character if you want to, said the priest.
Just ask the rock at the foot of Mt. Fuji.

I've since learned to enter rock with my breath.
I've always been fond of the hard.

***The Trouble with Yesterday is That it's Not
Today Even if it Plagiarizes Yesterday
It Won't Be the Same.***

Windows break because
they're glass. Flesh clearly isn't
iron. It never will be,
nor does it aspire such. A young

boy's boomerang is no weapon.
They'll kill him anyway.

Yesterday's headlines announced hope.
The trouble with hope
is that it shifts positions. Yoga

doesn't mean the body
bows like a field of wildflowers
in a bilingual downpour.

5. When the House Sleepwalks

I

Idle chatter in the dream and a matter of mice
spooning up spoils from the floor while dinner's
being made. If home's a ship that navigates
at night, who then is the dreamer, sheets akimbo,
as she fights to grasp something tangible?

II

Because the forgetful house sleepwalks to its boat
in the harbor, its owner has put the house's name
and address in its chimney pocket so the house won't get lost.

Once returned, the house assures its owner there will be
no more night wandering, but who can believe a dreamy
sleepwalker who tightens her sails before setting off?

Provisions

The cat meowed when the man opened his oyster tin. The feline rubbed against his leg. It seemed the calico bent her body with all her might into the man. The man liked this. It made him feel important—something he'd not recently felt.

As soon as the cat stopped, the man, again, stretched out his leg, shook it, "Here."

The scent of oysters teased the cat into believing *Perhaps I'll get some.* Oysters slid down the man's throat. On the tv tray by his recliner, he'd earlier set a six pack, two boxes of crackers and a second tin of smoked oysters.

This pleased the calico who saw in the man's feast her own feast. In no time the man finished off another beer, then rolled open his second can. The oysters slick in rich, golden oil.

The cat licked the rim of her hunger.

The man, before finishing his oysters, fell asleep, snored, his body occasionally jerking as though he were about to fall off a dock into the surprise of a cold lake.

The cat helped herself to the open tin, her whiskers pearly with oil.

I Dare You

to think of that mouse as someone capable of writing poetry, chewing on word choice, syntax, the crunch of meaning before it's absorbed, siphoning sound from nearby choices.

The mouse doesn't say, *I'm writer mouse. I'm special mouse.*

No, it chews on its pencil, shuffles paper, its optic nerve on fire deciding between sonnet or villanelle. It might even look up a word in the *Oxford English Dictionary, martini* or *mousetrap*, hoping to fully understand their derivation.

Or it could weigh the nearly imaginable while whiskers sweep scent, hopeful of Munster Cheese or Roquefort; but alas, the poem demands scrutiny, so a poet mouse must catch its muse before the trap snaps.

Oh, gluttony!

Birth Rights

How many times has a cat eloped with a dog
much to the chagrin of aunts and grandparents alike?

Sometimes a thing festers, all that's commonplace less so,
the newsfeed more contentious.

The dog might be in her igloo grinding up dream bones,
the cat soaking rays on the chaise.

For all we know or thought we knew
happiness walks barefoot summertime,

arms freely swinging. Don't be difficult, I tell myself
when attempting to reveal odd possibilities,

that present themselves fresh as plucked basil.
So, when the cat slapped the priest's signature

onto the marriage certificate, nabbed the dog and flew off
to Honolulu, don't be surprised that the pilot let each try their hand

(or paw, in this case,) at guiding *American Airlines* onto the landing strip
where the dark spread out its oilcloth, the cat, a mischievous look,

telling the dog, *A peach is a peach because it can't be an apple.*

Ever Since Her Friend's Drowning

1

The girl remembered bloodsuckers in the lake whenever she shoved her grandparent's rowboat out, how they latched onto her feet.

Terrified, she screamed for her mother. Her mother poured baking soda over her daughter's feet until one by one, the bloodsuckers dropped away. Afterwards, she ran scalding water over her feet, scrubbed them for hours.

At night, the girl dreamt that blood suckers burrowed into her arms and legs. She sucked her thumb and thrashed until her covers came undone.

Before bedtime, her mother rubbed pepper oil on her daughter's thumb to keep it from her mouth. But the girl licked off the oil and sucked her thumb harder.

Night after night the girl's room became the lake where the rowboat journeyed. Oars slurped as they dipped under. Stars cast lanterns on the water's surface.

2

The girl wondered how deep the lake, how vast its watery world. Hadn't she heard stories of a friend snatched by an underwater monster? Perhaps he was snagged in fishline, his mouth blowing empty bubbles, arms feathering currents.

None of her relatives knew for certain what took her playmate, although she heard them talk of strange sightings. The fact he'd never surfaced caused much speculation.

At night when she wasn't dreaming about bloodsuckers, she was dreaming about him, captive of the deep. They'd once worn goggles to swim out past the drop-off, but she never liked being in a place she couldn't see beneath.

She imagined a king bloodsucker, its cold body wrapped around her waist as though she were an arm for the leech's bold bracelet, her blood backing up, eyes bulging.

Ever since her friend's drowning, the girl never swam past the drop-off. She imagined stars sifting freckles onto his face, how his watery world would shimmer, his cuticles, crescent moons at the bottom of the lake.

Sheep Dance

The unemotional man lived with an emotional woman. She rode a carpet in her sleep, hoping to speed past a sleigh of stars. He counted sheep as they jumped over the fence, documented them in his leather-bound ledger.

Each solstice the woman made berries, rinsed them in rainwater collected in a galvanized pail set underneath the eaves. Her husband was wary of berries in winter, but ate them, nonetheless.

He dipped each one into a cup of cream. His milk lined lips aroused her, but nothing took his eyes off his ledger, his intent on amassing fortunes.

If sheep could bolt over fences with ease, then she, too, could hurdle the guard rail around him. But after much thought she decided that the only recourse was to leave, take up residence elsewhere.

On their last night together, she made a jar of berry wine. He slogged it down. So deep was his sleep that his ledger fell from his hand.

She and the sheep packed their bags and flew directly to France where they'd heard that the sheep dance festival was on, that sheepherders thought nothing of giving the old goat a swing, cloven hoofs tamping up a storm.

When a Day Trips You Up, Spits You Out

There are times when you go out into the world and everyone happily
greets you, and other days when even the post-mistress frowns,
chastising you—your mailings too bulky, poorly packaged,
another letter returned *Postage Due*. Even the lilacs by the post's
front door are rusted and droop like crumpled hankies.

Ok you say, I'll drive home, re-box what they wouldn't take. But
the new boxes balk at your stuffing them and perhaps you're trying
to fill what feels empty inside, the tape a tangled, sticky mess.

But not one to ever give up, not even on this poem that's undergone forty-five
rewrites, you hop in the car, your boxes and postage due money pocketed.
You just miss hitting a deer, trip on the steps, and when the post-mistress
sees you, she says: "Dear, you're a mess today. Your shirt's undone."

And the man standing nearby confirms she's right, and adds,
"But the view's great," and you gasp, realizing you don't have on a bra,
your shirt unbuttoned. Then back home that poem you've worked so hard on
dares you in its loudest, most obnoxious voice to toss it, start a new one.

Anne Sexton as a Hologram

> "Sometimes the soul takes pictures of things it has
> wished for, but never seen."
> —Anne Sexton

Before he lifts off her nightdress, Rilke
asks the countess for money to buy new writing journals,
his face, damp with intent. She sighs the sigh
of one amused, but slightly annoyed, responding *Rainier,*
why ask so much of me? He seals her mouth
with kisses, not so much to get her mind off his request,
but to assure himself of a more high-minded purpose—the poems.

Worried Rilke sees me, I thin myself to the faintest outline,
reload my camera, snuff out my cigarette.
I remain hidden behind the countess's mirror stand,
where I listen intently to his whispers,

You, and only you, remain my dearest.

2.

Keats, too, has intoxicating words, Fanny drunk on the idea
of him. When I stand at the foot of his bed
at Wentworth Place, his hand dreaming of her breast,
his angel face lit with the thought of her, at first, I think a madman
in his sleep. It's a blessing, given life's turmoil,
that Keats knows nothing of his brother's impending plight,
how sickness soaks the living. He sleep-talks to Fanny, "Your beauty
grows upon me and I feel a greater love through all my essence steal"

3.

Hemingway wasn't easy to observe, his renowned restlessness,
constant waking murderous on my nerves,
yet I arrived safely at 74 rue du Cardinal Lemoine,
a small walk-up, where I found both Hadley and Ernest
in sexual congress, he madly driving his bull horn. Once asleep
his hands became fists. He perhaps dreamt of a rope around his neck
because he fiercely tugged at his nightshirt's collar.

*Stay asleep dear Hemingway Anne says, you've struggled enough.
There's no bulls in your room. Not yet.*

For the Dancing Birds

Little Monk, I call my desk, as I caress its shiny surface.

It happily groans. We have worked like this
for many years. What it likes best
is a certain quiet that rises,

how thoughts become dancing birds,
and the writer at the desk,
a wide-open sky.

Tree Burial

Already my bones are breaking for our trees—how
They drop, branches ripped free—

That sonorous thud only a ponderosa makes as it's felled—already
There's empty space where they once stood,
Sky sweepers, home to robins, granary to acorn woodpeckers

Already my temperature rises with loss of their shade,
And from the music they made in wind, their gentle pluck

Across cords of pine needles, the swish
That lulls me to sleep   O, my friends of both sky and earth
You'll be missed,
And the owl that made its home in the crux of your limbs asks Who

When I am Dead and Shelved

in a dank grave, be my historian and write
of my life on earth, its apples and blossoms,
how any existence builds from blunders, the cryptic
sanctity of fault turned blessing, the detritus of sorrow,
so many burials, and one that hit hardest,
she whose coffined hands I tried to pull apart
to cup my face, but no, she remained
ice-stiff—dear Ella—who raised me
from the dead when childhood horror
dragged the sleeping self of myself under
& into the world of demons no child knew existed,
but that, now, in retrospect, a small chapter
of this passage called growth upon the born
which may or may not take hold, one death making
all deaths possible, my own in New Hampshire,
where I waitressed at Crawford Notch,
my soul at the window looking back on my bedded self,
but no, I didn't die then, not until later, much later
when love so terribly blinding, so fierce,
burned me at the stake of desire, his hand
a branding iron, my body a disciple of affection
so radiant it became the heart as claimed,
still, through the years of absence, I sharpened
my longing to shape-shift into the future,
leaving me breathless at the door of all remembering.

What's dark remains dark

Someone shot me with a thought.

It entered my head.

It bled and bled.
Blood becomes you, someone said.

The bullet felt like cool lake water.

I shot it back at the one
who shot it at me.

He became a leaf cat saddled
with a full rucksack.

Can a Voice be Promiscuous?

I once loved a man nearly large as Diego Rivera,
his voice lyrical as mountain streams,

not like Leonard Cohen's, more
like the velvet of an Andrea Bocelli,

a voice you could cape yourself in
on cold, lonely nights, a voice that meant

heaven's angels wouldn't go on strike.
Today's longing returns his voice

with poignancy and again
I'm straddled across him, knees

riding the belly sides of his breath,
hair curtained over his face,

rivers of breath breaking.
Oh, love, why didn't we remain together,

mark our years with steppingstones
alongside that river where first we stepped?

To Measure Love with a Yardstick

There were stars. There was walking with a lover.
There was a glance, a whisper, Should we?
There was a jaunt towards a local B&B,
a door opening onto a room. A question,
Dare we? There was flesh upon flesh,
no hesitation, no going back. There was
a voice that sang as it slid down my ears,
a sweetness that still haunts me. It tasted
of honey and sounded like St. Cecilia's Mass.
It was holy. There were stars burning
at the edge of hearing, a stroke of tenderness.
There was a reluctant Goodbye my love,
I can't return. Nevertheless, much remained.
A heart filled with love, a yardstick well trained.

The Opening World

Once thirst is quenched,
where do I go into the opening world?

(There's no place to turn me away.)

If my feet sing as I stroll
do not look strangely upon me.

    Who could have known
that my feet would sip from streams,

or that my toes would play tag in the shoe of traveler earth?

At the Slightest

What was the leaf cat but a promise of seasons,
sunshine and rain, sometimes snow?

When the leaf cat prowled forests
animals tucked in their chins.

How could they have known their visitor
was a figment of their imagination,

a thing that scuttles off at the slightest provocation?
Forsake the tooth fairy, forsake S and his elves,

what's real is magical enough and makes its appearance
when the body's close to breaking, eyes tear-welled,

and the heart, its lonely tether, about to seek splendor in wreckage.

Acknowledgments

Autumn Sky Poetry Daily, 2018: "Blood Relative"

Adirondack Review, "New England Farmhouse," Nominated for a Pushcart

Artemis Journal 2023: "The One with Violets in Her Lap," "The Whacking Stick," "Summons"

Blue Fifth Review: "All summer I've waited for…"

Blue Heron Review, 2024: In the Collage of my Mind/I'm a Simple Design" Nominated for Pushcart

California Quarterly, Volumes 40 & 41: "When the House Sleepwalks," "When a Day Trips You Up, Spits You Out," "Window Magic"

Folkways Press, LLC, 2024: "Fold Your Tears into Peace Signs,"

January Review, 2020: "Birth Rights"

The Lake, UK: "Fish Hatchery"

MacQueens Quinterly, "The Star Drum," The Easel, the Leather Coat & the Blue Grass Perfume" "Lovely that Black Crow Grandmother Brought into the Camp," "Ultrasound," "My Heart's no Casual Affair"

MockingHeart Review, 2023: "The Christening Stone," "Already"

Naugatuck River Review, 2019: "From the Northeast Kingdom," "Where have all the Fishermen Gone?"

New American Poetry: "The Leaf Cat"

New Verse News: "The Trouble With Yesterday is That It's Not Today Even of it Plagiarizes Yesterday"

New Village Press 2023, Editor Leigh Sugar, a compilation by writers who taught in prisons. That's a Pretty Thing to Call It: "To Nuance or

Not to Nuance," "Prison Portrait"

Poet News: "My Face Washed Away in the Rain"

Red Rock Review, 2016: "Near the Now," The Solitude," "Magic Powder," "Plate of Stone"

Sequestrum, 2019; "To Ask a Question Does Not Mean You Get an Answer"

South Dakota Review, "Glass Garden Cloche," "Skillet Offerings," "Luxury" Now entitled "Whiteout"

The Power of the Feminine Vol.II 2024: "The Day My Fallopian Tubes Asked/Me to Play Hop-Scotch," & "Missing You"

Trag, a Serbian Journal, 2016, "Search"

Tule Review, 2023: "The Animals Will Indict Us"

VerseVirtual, 2023: "The Thick," "For the Love of Doorknobs"

Visions International, 2024: "At the Goodbye Door"

Voices, 2023, also in *The Way to my Heart*, edited by Kelly Ann Jacobson, 2017: "*Trolling the Unknown*" & "*Anne Sexton as a Hologram*"

WORDPEACE, Summer of 2022 & 2025: "Vice" & "Being in a Solitary Frame of Mind"

Women in a Golden State, 2025: "The day my fallopian tubes asked me to play hopscotch"

Worth More Standing, Poets and Activists Pay Homage to Trees, 2022: "Tree Burial"

Your Daily Poem: "Embers"

Books: *The Tenderness House*, "Poet's Corner Press," 2004: *The Broken Bone Tongue*, "Black Buzzard Press," 2009: *Cathedral of the Hand*, "Finishing Line Press," 2016, *Camaraderie of the Marvelous*, 2021, "Kelsay Books."

"Scent of Solitude" nominated in 2025 for a Pushcart prize by *Blue Heron Review*

Thanks to The California Council for the Humanities Stories Project for a grant that funded poetry workshops at the Rancheria in Susanville where I worked with Maidu, Pit River, Washoe and the Northern Paiute Tribes. Also thanks to the California Arts Council for their "Artists in the Schools Residency," funded, in part, by The National Endowment for the Arts and The William James Association's Prison Arts Program as well as California Poets in the School.

Dianna MacKinnon Henning taught through California Poets in the Schools, received several California Arts Council grants and taught poetry workshops through the William James Association's Prison Arts Program, including Folsom Prison, Diamond View Middle School and runs "The Thompson Peak Writers' Workshop." Publications, in part: Naugatuck River Review 2025; *Women in a Golden State*, 2025; *Visions* 2025; *The Power of the Feminine*, Vol. II 2024; *One Art Poetry*, 2024; Folkways Press; *Mocking Heart Review,* 2024; *Poet News,* Sacramento; *Worth More Standing, Poets and Activists Pay Homage to Trees; Voices; Artemis Journal,* 2021 & 2022 & 2023; *The Adirondack Review; Memoir Magazine;The Tule Review; The Lake, UK; California Quarterly; The Plague Papers, Blue Heron Review,* and *New American Writing.* Nomination by *The Adirondack Review* for a Pushcart Prize a few years back. MFA in Writing '89, Vermont College. Recently nominated by *Blue Heron Review* for a Pushcart for her poem "In the Collage of my Mind/I'm a Simple Design," her ninth Pushcart nomination 2024. She has a new book "Rucksacks for the Leaf Cat" by Finishing Line Press due out Jan. 2026. Book publications, *Poets Corner Press, Black Buzzard Press, Finishing Line Press & Kelsay Books.* Website: www.diannahenning.com

www.ingramcontent.com/pod-product-compliance
Lightning Source LLC
Chambersburg PA
CBHW030054170426
43197CB00010B/1520